MW01073669

269 *Amazing* SEX TIPS & TRICKS FOR HIM

ANNE HOOPER
PHILLIP HODSON

SOURCEBOOKS CASABLANCA™
AN IMPRINT OF SOURCEBOOKS, INC.®
NAPERVILLE, ILLINOIS

First published in Great Britain in 2001 by Robson Books, The Chrysalis Building, Bramley
Road, London W10 6SP, a member of the Chrysalis BooksGroup. © 2001 Anne Hooper and
Phillip Hodson

Published by Sourcebooks Casablanca, an imprint of Sourcebooks, Inc.
P.O. Box 4410, Naperville, Illinois 60567-4410
(630) 961-3900
Fax: (630) 961-2168
www.sourcebooks.com

Library of Congress Cataloging-in-Publication Data

Hooper, Anne

  269 amazing sex tips and tricks for him / by Anne Hooper and Phillip Hodson.
    p. cm.
  Rev. ed. of: 269 amazing sex tips and tricks for men. c2003.
  Includes bibliographical references and index.
  1. Sex instruction for men. 2. Sexual excitement. I. Hodson, Phillip. II. Hooper, Anne- 269
amazing sex tips and tricks for men. III. Title. IV. Title: Two hundred sixty-nine amazing sex
tips and tricks for him.
  HQ36.H658 2009
  613.9'6081--dc22

                              2009030708

CONTENTS

1: a real man 1

2: tricks to tempt and tantalize her 27

3: tricks to tempt and tantalize you 67

4: vibes, lubes, and sex toys 89

5: sextremes 109

6: sexopoly 121

about the authors 154

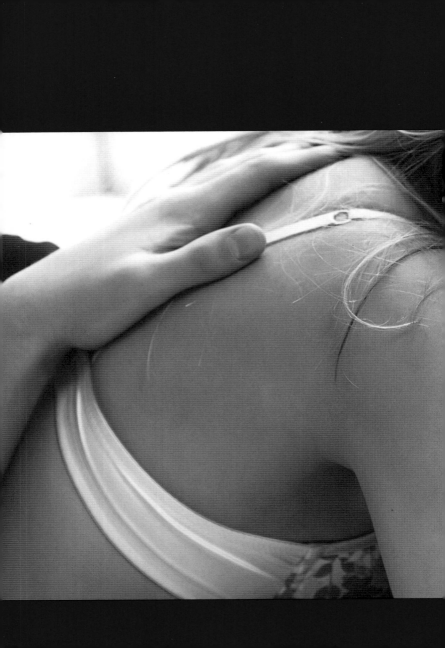

one | A REAL MAN

BE *unashamed*

1. Don't feel apologetic for your shape, size, or physical appearance.

2. Feel normal, even if by some standards you think you are not. It's the human being inside you that counts.

3. Fetishes: the most well-adjusted male fetishists we know are completely happy with their fetish and open about their interests.

4. This means that it doesn't matter what your lawful sexual interests are—it's YOU, your personality, that attracts (or doesn't attract) your woman.

5. But don't be vulgar. Research shows that although many men are excited by "filth," women are repelled. The sooner you get rid of anger and crudity, the more success you'll have.

real SEX DIFFERENCES

Research shows that there ARE some real sex differences between men and women (although in most respects, the two sexes are astoundingly similar).

6. Men are visual—they are actively turned on by what they SEE. This means that they don't have to lift a muscle to get an erection—just looking does most of it for them. Be unashamed of your frankly erotic reactions.

unreal
SEX DIFFERENCES

What you learn is not quite the same as what you innately inherit. Men are more comfortable with their bodies, their genitals, and masturbation from a much earlier age than women. This is because men's sexual apparatus is positioned on the body where it can be easily located, even by a child of two. (Actually, it is easily located even earlier than that. Studies of baby boys have shown that quite tiny babies discover the joys of genital pleasure.) Boys get tons of practice at sex (with themselves) and gain an advantage over women there. And most societies in history have been less disapproving of boys' sexual curiosity.

There have been innumerable surveys of penis size, from the famous Kinsey Report to the infamous *Forum* magazine, so there is a fair consensus of "normality."

7 Eight or more inches is really big, but truthfully not better. It may fill up your woman satisfactorily, but if she is built small, you are also likely to be crashing into the far end of her cervix and causing serious pain or even womb displacement. Go for the doggy position or ask her to sit on top so she can control the depth of thrust. Remember that the average length of the human vagina is only six inches.

8 Two-and-a-half inches is small, but because the owners of these mini crown jewels have to put a little extra into stimulating their women, they are often the best lovers of the lot.

THE *average* PENIS

The normal range of penis size is from two-and-a-half inches to ten. Around five-and-a-half to six inches is the American and European average, although please note that penis size depends on the body type you inherit from your native ancestors. In the Far East, for example, where men inherit slim body size, the average can be as much as two inches less.

9   Warning: make sure your condoms fit BEFORE your sex tryst. Find the size that fits you properly. In Thailand, where penises aren't as big as those in the West, they only size condoms in superlatives—Jumbo, Colossal, and Super-Colossal.

GET THE MOST
OUT OF *your genitals*

Lubrication inside the penile passage is provided by the Cowper's gland (inside the body). The penile shaft is filled with spongy tissue that fills up with blood during sexual excitement, thus producing an erection. The foreskin is the penis's natural protective wrapper. The glans is the head of the penis and exquisitely responsive. The scrotum is a carrying case for your balls (testicles) and keeps them at optimum temperature so that your valuable sperm get the best possible chance to score a hit. The perineum is the highly sensitive area between the back of the scrotum and the anus. The anus is densely packed with erogenous feeling.

10 Consider taking muira puama—extracted from the Brazilian rain forest tree of the same name. Muira puama appears to increase blood flow in general and penis blood flow in particular. Dr. Jacques Waynberg of the Institute of Sexology in Paris says muira puama is one of the best herbs for sustaining optimal sexual performance.

One theory has it that muira puama contains a substance (beta sitosterol) that activates the body's receptors for hormones such as testosterone. The better the hormone works within our bodies, the higher the sex drive and performance we are likely to reach. An added bonus is that muira puama also guards against rheumatism, which is a double bonus for those wanting to continue their sex lives until they drop.

11 Eat your oatmeal every day.

In 1986, the Institute for the Advanced Study of Human Sexuality conducted a double-blind crossover study of men and women where some were given a wild oats formula to eat. A large portion of men reported increased sex drive, firmer erections, and increased sexual pleasure when taking the formula. Women reported increased sexual desire, increased sexual fantasy, and more vigorous pursuit of sexual fulfillment.

Theory behind the extraordinary oats? Dr. Ted McIlvenna reckons the plant possesses an enzyme that helps unbind testosterone from other substances in the body, thus giving the hormone a much greater aphrodisiac effect.

12 Get on the ginseng.

A new scientific examination of the fabulously reputed substance ginseng shows it to be an "adaptogen," that is, it helps you adapt to circumstances. If you are tired, ginseng will energize you. If you are overly anxious, ginseng will calm you down. But ginseng's most famous use is for enhancing sexual response and performance in both men and women. Chinese tests of ginseng show that it:

○ Increases production of luteinizing hormone, which in turn stimulates the production of progesterone.

○ Improves muscle development and increases stamina.

○ Increases testosterone secretion in men and women—testosterone is now believed to be the main hormone responsible for sex drive and performance.

13 Sorry guys, this isn't just nagging. If you want to be the ultimate sex machine with the hardest cock and the longest performance, you need to back off:

○ Tobacco

○ Alcohol

○ Pot

They really do screw up your sex life. Beer is particularly bad news for penises (brewer's droop is real) and the prostate gland. A Hawaiian study of more than 6,500 men over a period of seventeen years showed that it only takes three bottles of beer a month for men to develop prostate problems. This is because the beer increases the levels of a hormone called prolactin. Prolactin is also commonly associated with flagging sexual interest and performance. Also: two high-tar cigarettes smoked one after the other will swiftly reduce blood flow into the penis by up to one-third.

IT'S *what you do with it* THAT COUNTS

The imaginative lover uses his penis for much more than sexual intercourse. Try thinking of the penis:

14. As a massage stick—using a hand to guide it, plus a lot of massage oil, experiment with rolling your penis around your lover's body. The bonus is it feels fantastic for you as well as for her.

15. As a vibrator—manipulating your penis with your hand, use it to drum against her clitoris—women adore it.

16. As a sneaky snake—if your penis has an overpowering inclination to nestle within your woman's crevices, be these the armpit, between the breasts, or between the clefts of her buttocks, give in to the innocent, wild creature.

If the gypsy in you is longing to spread your seed, you'll be happy to know that there are methods of boosting the powers of the aforesaid seed.

17 Try eating foods rich in zinc—these include seeds and nuts. Adequate zinc is vital for the production of testosterone, for sperm formation, and for prostate health. So knock back a large handful of pumpkin seeds every day!

CUSTOM-FLAVORED
semen

Hoping for a lot of oral sex? Which, naturally, she will be gasping for? Better aim at improving the smell and taste of your semen as an allurement.

18 Cut down on the pepper and salt—these make semen taste bitter.

19 Go for blander food such as french fries and peas for a "neutral" odor.

20 Eat cinnamon and sugar for a sweeter tang.

THE WELL-GROOMED *penis*

The fashion-conscious penis knows that if it wishes to attract women of superior quality, it needs to look good. Good grooming means:

21   Shampoo and set. It's cool to be clean.

22   Hair styling. Using razor and scissors, go for V-shaped, heart-shaped, or inverted pyramid-shaped pubes.

23   Smooth to touch—take a tip from African men and oil your wand—experiment with good stuff from The Body Shop, for instance.

FLEXI-COCK

Want the world's strongest and most flexible penis? Try Kegel exercises (anal-buttock muscle clenches). These consist of:

24. Twitching the penis ten times a session at least three times a day.

25. Raising your cock by degrees, as if you were erecting it in stages. Try pulling your cock up to 1) a low stage, 2) a medium height, and then 3) the summit. Then let it down again in the reverse sequence.

26. Ultimate test. Hang a tea towel on your penis and keep the towel horizontal for five minutes.

TROUBLE
achieving...

27 If you are over forty-five, you could be forgiven for reaching for the Viagra. Some men use this recreationally, but be warned, this is dangerous if you have a heart condition. Never mix Viagra with any other nitrite substance.

28 Remember, Viagra can take up to an hour to work, and nothing will happen unless you engage in foreplay.

29 Cialis is the newer, longer-acting anti-impotence drug. It may be effective for up to thirty-seven hours (if you have a free day). A similar drug is Levitra.

30 Below age forty-five, the problem is more likely to be psychological (always get a health exam to be sure). Remember, it is normal for all men to lose their erection sometimes—even James Bond once had impotence!

31 Cock rings or bands around the base of the penis can be helpful in cases of psychological erectile disorder.

32 Here's a piece of insider advice from movie star Cary Grant: "To succeed with the opposite sex, tell her you're impotent. She can't wait to disprove it."

to snip
OR NOT TO SNIP

A fierce battle has raged, probably since the beginning of time, on the merits of the circumcised versus the uncircumcised penis.

Circumcision: merits

- Hygiene: prevents inflammation and painful swelling due to infection under the foreskin.

- Believed to reduce possibility of transmitting sexual disease and of receiving it.

- If you are a premature ejaculator, circumcision may slow you down—a little.

Circumcision: demerits

- You will never look the same again.

- You may desensitize your penis.

- It's a painful experience.

- Cosmetic surgery for reconstruction is expensive and isn't very effective.

General view: it probably doesn't matter much either way.

two TRICKS TO TEMPT AND TANTALIZE HER

THE ALL-OVER *body orgasm*

33 Learn to link her genital excitement with the rest of her skin. Don't make the mistake of thinking her only erotic area lies between the legs.

34 As you stroke and rub her clitoris, always stroke some other part of her body at the same time. You might try connecting the clitoris up with the:

35 Breasts

36 Toes

37 Mouth

38 Anus

39 Armpits

These other areas will get so tuned in to eroticism that they will grow to share it!

SEDUCTION IS FOR
THE *other person*

40   Don't automatically do to your woman what you would like done to you. Her erogenous zones are not yours—they are different. And every person differs from the rest. So think about what would be good for her.

If you don't know what this is, try following this suggested sequence:

41   Hug and caress.

42   Kiss first lightly and then passionately.

43   As you undress, spend ages cuddling and stroking and hugging close.

44   Only toward the end of this all-over body pleasure graduate to touching her genitals.

45   Do not go for intercourse without having first stroked her clitoris into excitement.

46 If your woman is not ready to get so intimate with you, she will resist. Don't be discouraged if she retreats or pushes you aside.

47 Enjoy the challenge of discovering her way of thinking so that you can assess what feels right (and sexy) to her. Best advice is to make touch gradual, not to rush things. Be prepared sometimes to take days, even weeks, getting close.

48 Passionate kissing goes a long way toward dissolving resistance.

49 Warning: don't confuse her signals of reluctance and inexperience with real signals of not wanting sex. Never force someone nor get her drunk nor try to take advantage.

play with
HER HEAD

Ways of provoking her interest in getting closer to you are:

50 Seem vulnerable yourself.

51 Be passive and putty in her hands.

52 Be interested in her one day and, when she has clearly responded, play hard to get the next.

53 Be seen to be attractive to other women.

54 Seem sexually confident (especially when it's less than true).

MAKING PATTERNS—
WITH *lubricant*

55 When your lover, thanks to your powers of touch, has become a quivering bundle of finely tuned nerves, this is the time to remember the powers of lubrication. If you don't believe there are differences between being touched by a dry hand and being touched by a wet one, experiment on yourself. A wet hand slipping around your genitals is incredibly sensuous.

56 Masturbating with a dry hand is one of the first parts of the exercise to overcome premature ejaculation—you are least likely to let rip at such a time of drought.

THE CLITORIS—
an exposé

The clitoris is a large organ extending either side and beneath the vaginal lips so that most of it tends to be hidden from view. This means that a few women don't even know it is there (not to mention a lot of men). But this doesn't mean it ISN'T there.

57 Learn to recognize its small, bud-like shape, so you can find the tip of the clitoris. This swells on excitement just like a penis does—though the result is less visible. Once it is seriously excited, the tip proves disconcerting because it appears to disappear.

58 You can find it by pulling back the pubic mound with one hand and exposing the flesh. This stretching sensation will also feel extremely erotic to its owner.

59 Very gentle rubbing on an exposed clitoral bud is sensational.

LET YOUR HAND
feel pleasure

60 If you find manual foreplay boring, tune in to the sensations your own hand is receiving as it carries out its labor of love. All touch can feel erotic, and you will find as you vary the pressure you are giving that the variation affects your experience, too. The hand is one of the most sensual parts of the human anatomy, since it is packed with nerve endings.

Touch can make you feel:

○ Profound friendship

○ Affection

○ Sensuality

○ Eroticism

Of course a limp penis matters to YOU. But it doesn't matter as much as you think.

61 It is normal for erection to come and go during lengthy lovemaking. Don't think there is something wrong. There isn't.

62 If you are a master of the fingertips, capable of making your partner's body feel on fire, your penis won't matter.

63 If you have real problems with mild impotence, women actually enjoy helping their men to climax. Women love a challenge!

IT'S OK TO
take a break

64. If sex feels like a major performance, i.e., that you must constantly appear on top of things (especially her), relax. It's OK to take breaks. What's more, it actually gives the two of you time to rest. Sometimes you need this in order to feel truly open with each other.

know
HER EXCITEMENT

65 If this sounds over-simple, bear in mind that some men still think a woman is sexually excited when she begins to vaginally lubricate. Real excitement consists of far more. For starters, different women need different excitement triggers. It's your task to find out what suits your woman best.

66 Try a little clitoral massage.

67 Dirty stories whispered in her ear may be just what she wants.

68 General all-over adoration and worship for two days beforehand can make for a truly delightful denouement.

69 There comes a stage when your woman looks out of it. She's away in her head somewhere. This can be disconcerting. But don't, whatever you do, try to recapture her attention. When she looks like this, it is because she is so focused on the pleasure you are giving her that she has literally entered a different brain state. Far from being distracted, she is paying you the ultimate compliment. She can only get to such a peak of orgasmic balance when she feels incredibly safe and incredibly stimulated. And it is YOU who is doing the stimulating. So feel good—for yourself, too.

best times
OF THE MONTH

Women, being the fascinating and varied creatures that they are, are not always in exactly the same mood every time when it comes to sex. Like men, they are subject to the same health problems, stresses, and fatigues. Unlike men, they are also subject to their monthly hormonal cycles. This means that there are particular days in each menstrual cycle when she feels much sexier than others. The sexier days tend to be in:

70 The five to ten days following her period.

71 The middle of the month for a couple of days only, when she is ovulating.

72 The day (or couple of days) immediately before her period. This is often a dynamite time for lovemaking.

73 Make a mental note (or even a written one) of your partner's menstrual cycle for a couple of months to gain a good idea of her sexual timing.

74 Studies of men and women affected by SAD (seasonal affective disorder) reveal that there are two peaks for depression brought on by the time of year. Depressive peaks are in winter and (more surprisingly) summer. This means that if you want to go for the optimal times for amazing sex, you should make the most of spring and autumn.

THUMBELINA
dance

And all the rest of your fingers, too. Here's how you perform the Symphony of the Roving Finger and Thumb. Using tons of lube:

75 Stretch your hand across and lightly rub and stroke the insides of her thighs. Bring your hands toward her genitals each time and brush them lightly before going back to the knee again.

76 Brush with your whole hand up across her labia toward the pubic mound. Do not be rough. Make these moves slowly. Deliberately linger.

77 Let one of your fingers (or thumb) "accidentally" glance inside the labia so that it skims the entrance to the vagina and brushes inside the pubic area, bumping against the clitoris on the way up. Repeat several times.

GO FOR HER
g-spot

78 Your woman's G-spot (if she has one—not every woman does) will be on the upper wall of the vagina, probably a long way back. It helps if you possess long musicians' fingers! The latest theory is that the G-spot is the clitoral root, the very base of the clitoris. Whatever! It feels like a small swelling.

79 To obtain sensual feeling, press down on the G-spot with the pads of the finger(s), occasionally lightening then strengthening the pressure. The G-spot responds better to steady pressure than it does to rubbing.

GO FOR
her clit

80 Focusing your finger more specifically, pull it up against the underside of the clitoral bud and let it bump across the top surface.

81 Using a highly-lubricated forefinger only, delicately saw at one side of the clitoral tip, up and down.

82 Do the same on the other side.

83 Gently rim around the clitoral head with a fingertip (short fingernails only).

84 Gently rim in the opposite direction. These strokes can be done with the main part of the finger held away from the clitoris, then with the main part of the finger right up against the clitoral tip.

85 Circle directly on the clitoral tip, so lightly that you are barely touching.

tongue TORTURE

86 Always use the tip of the tongue in an upward movement, and lick from the entrance of the vagina up and over the clitoral tip, repeatedly, in short strokes.

87 Try licking first to one side...

88 Then to the other.

89 Then over the top of the clitoris itself.

90 Pointing the tongue, twirl it gently around the clitoris clockwise...

91 Then counter-clockwise.

further TONGUE TORTURE

92 Using the tip of the tongue, push gently and repeatedly on to one side of the clitoral tip...

93 On to the other...

94 On to the tip.

95 Combine gentle sucking with these strokes.

96 If one or more strokes prove especially effective, stay with these. Once something takes off erotically, women prefer repetition until they reach orgasm.

97 Men's mistakes: the delicate bud of the clitoris is not as robust as the penis. Don't touch it too quickly or too hard. If you touch or suck too hard, she gets desensitized—NOT what you want.

getting to know
YOUR LOVER'S BODY

Not all good communication is verbal. Our question is: "Could you pass a test on how your lover likes to be touched?" You couldn't? Take time out for some serious homework:

98 Ask—it's the oldest method, but it works.

99 Trial and error—watch for signs that some strokes cause her serious bliss. Repeat them.

100 Get her to show you how by putting her hands on top of yours.

101 Experiment with new caresses. It's like fashion: some styles won't work; some become classics. But you have to try.

102 Learn her time cycle—by which we mean, how soon does she want each caress to move to someplace more intense, and how long would she rather wait before it does?

103   If she says something useful like "When you touch me on the arm (or the back of the knee or my neck), it makes my vagina tingle," treat this as very helpful information.

104   Find out what sorts of touch pressure she likes.

105   Do you know what sequence of caresses she prefers? If not, remember that old episode of *Friends* where the girls explain they don't always enjoy going from kissing to breast manipulation to stroking between the legs to sex—they like to "mix things up."

106   Build a "mental body map" of your partner. Color the hot spots in red in your head. Commit this to memory.

107   Try something new every time. Kiss her wrist or inside her elbow, behind her ear, inside her thigh. See if you can make her purr.

Pay special attention to the traditional erogenous zones. They can be so tricky. Funny thing: hardly any two women like them stroked in the same way. In fact, most women protest that men are:

108 Too rough on nipples.

109 Too quick to touch the exposed clitoral head.

110 And they use the clitoris as if it wanted to be jerked off like a penis or erased by a tongue when it doesn't. Only she can say; you should obey.

111 Good communication also recognizes life's emotional-sexual links. By this we mean:

112 Foreplay begins at breakfast—don't expect a warm reception if you've been like a bear with a sore head all day.

113 Sometimes women need love in order to want sex.

114 Sometimes you will need sex in order to express your love.

115 But sometimes everybody is a bit confused about how they feel and what they want; so keep an open mind when your overtures don't always succeed. Perhaps she needs to laugh a bit first? So lighten things up:

116 Play a comedy tape.

117 Watch an emotional movie and cuddle.

118 Offer to massage her feet with aromatherapy oil (and after thirty minutes, cheat a bit by slipping your fingers up her legs).

119 Give her warm spicy wine to drink. (It heats the important parts.)

120 Play with her hair and tell her how much you like her scent (or perfume or smell—whichever term you can risk), but the idea is to connect to her core earthiness.

kiss AND MAKE UP

Communication includes what to do when it breaks down (as it will). So when you argue, don't ruin your relationship. After a fight, try these:

121 The magic 5-to-1 ratio: make sure there is five times as much positive touching between you and your partner as there is negative feeling.

122 Remove blame from your comments.

123 Say how you feel.

124 Listen to your partner.

125 Don't criticize or try to analyze your partner's personality.

126 Don't insult, mock, or use sarcasm.

127 Be direct and stick with one situation rather than dragging up the past.

128 Learn how to calm yourself when floods of emotion block communication. Discuss how you can take a break.

129 Think of your partner's good qualities—praise and admire them.

130 Look at these principles again and again. It takes a long time to learn new habits.

three TRICKS TO
TEMPT AND
TANTALIZE YOU

STOP YOURSELF
FROM *coming*

You're only a third of the way into glorious sex and suddenly you perceive it is all about to explode—far too soon. Here's what you do:

131 Grasp your penis head around the coronal ridge with finger and thumb and squeeze—HARD. This prevents the ejaculate from leaving the penis and forces your sexual response to go back a step.

132 Or, if you are seriously into fucking, reach around behind you and, grasping your balls, firmly pull down with your hand so that once again you block the tubes.

133 Tao practitioners place a forefinger on a certain spot on the perineum and press firmly to prevent ejaculation. We suggest you practice this one in private first!

134 If you are into serious restriction, you'll like this. You take elastic surgical cord (emphatically NOT a rubber band that would cut into the flesh), and tie it around the head of the penis while it is still erect. When your mate sucks on you, you will get excited beyond endurance because your penis will literally be unable to go down.

135 Safety warning: as with any kind of bondage, NEVER leave your lover (or yourself) tied up for longer than half an hour. A warning sign is when your penis goes purple.

MARSHMALLOW
delight

136 Persuade your lovely partner to fill her mouth with marshmallow, which your penis will experience as soft and squishy.

surgical
GLOVES

137 Ask her to don a pair of surgical gloves before doing unspeakable things to your genitals by way of "medical" examination.

HEALTH *charm*

In case there are any men out there who still believe it is unhealthy to masturbate, please be aware that some doctors think:

138 Regular masturbation drains the body of seminal fluid, thereby helping the individual avoid congestive prostatitis.

139 If the penis is not used regularly (so that it "remembers" how to get excited, get erect, and retain erection), the erection mechanism might get "rusty" and, at a later date, find it difficult to start again.

The Kinsey Report described one individual who masturbated twenty-three times a week. Amazingly enough, he still retained his hearing and his eyesight, and he did not succumb regularly to the flu.

Viva, the 1970s U.S. supermodel, described in her autobiography how she and her lover set out to break the world record for orgasms. She found after two-and-a-half days in bed that she could not continue. Her body seemed to have gone on strike.

Kinsey also recorded the case of one man who had three orgasms a day over a period of thirty years and another who averaged 33.1 orgasms a week over a thirty-year period. However, Kinsey also found that the younger you were, the more likely you were to experience successive orgasms.

OUT-OF-BODY
experience

Sexiest choices for the most exciting place in which to have oral sex or mutual masturbation include:

140 Under the blanket on your plane trip.

141 In the bathroom during your train ride.

142 In the back of your car, while parked in the local scenic spot.

143 On the kitchen table.

144 À la Richard Gere—on a grand piano.

Serious warning: it is (often) illegal to have sex in public places, so please be exceedingly careful or wait until you get home.

PUTTING OFF
THE *heavenly moment*

Many people believe that you experience orgasm much more profoundly if you forgo having an orgasm on at least two out of three lovemaking episodes.

145 Mentally, you are said to desire sex much more strongly.

146 Emotionally, when orgasm does arrive you are more likely to be deeply moved.

147 Physically, the final release will be cataclysmic by comparison with routine climax.

At least, that's the PR version. Not one for impatient lovers.

148 Fill her mouth with toothpaste or brandy as she gives you fellatio.

149 Suck on a strong mint while doing likewise.

150 Place her finger and thumb in a ring to her mouth and then use the ring as an outer part of her mouth while she gives you oral sex. The advantage is that she can contract her digits to give you a tighter fit.

151 Use her free hand to stroke as many parts of you as she can find while having intercourse. She might aim at the thighs, the buttocks, underneath the testicles, twirling your nipples, or into the anus.

Provided your woman gives you her complete agreement, go for anal sex. Best ways to do this are:

152 To lubricate your penis and her anus liberally.

153 To work on widening her anus with your forefinger. When you can get so that you can fit at least two fingers into it, this is the time to slip your penis in.

154 If she goes into a spasm, just wait, moving only enough to keep your erection.

155 It takes time to stretch open enough to let the experience become painless. Do not rush things.

PROLONGING YOUR
orgasm

You might:

156   Withdraw from intercourse just before the point of no return, only going back to it a little later.

157   Go into slow motion mode just before ejaculation. Slow all body movements.

158   Restrain the testicles by hand; holding them away from the body.

159 Provoke a quickie. You strip naked; she remains clothed.

160 Get her to leave her panties on during sex.

161 Challenge her to make you hard without touching your penis at all. A clue: if she mouths the words, "I want you inside me please," but doesn't come near you, you'll find that helps!

162 When she has removed her bra, take her head in your hands and place her ear right over your heart so that she can hear its beat and listen to your desire.

MORE
erotic treats

163 Ask her to gently pinch your nipples, trying out softer and harder clamps. Give her feedback on how hard you would really like it.

164 Ask her to wedge her vibrator in between you as you have intercourse. Then use it to make her come while you are still inside her.

165 Suggest she puts lipstick around the head of your penis and next sucks it off.

166 Ask her to take her clothes off and sit on a chair at the opposite side of the room. Next ask her to masturbate, promising her that you will not move from where you are seated. Then honor the promise.

four | VIBES, LUBES, AND SEX TOYS

VIBES— *the very latest* MODELS

There's a small revolution going on in the sex-toys industry. Vibrators are being transformed as a result of the fabulous new materials now available. They are soft, malleable, and feel like real skin in fun materials such as see-through translucent jellies and gorgeous jewel-like colors. Here are some of the best, many of which can be found on the top vibrator website on the Internet, www.goodvibes.com.

VIBES *for you*

167 Ecsta-Sleeve Vulva. A stretchable sleeve made of cyber-skin that fits over the penis and includes a vibrating egg for stimulating the sensitive head of the penis.

168 Ball Collar. This attaches around the testicles and you can then add weights to it.

169 Neptune Ring Vibe. This is a tiny vibrating dolphin attached to a cock ring. This works either by giving your lover a solo buzz or by stimulating the clitoris during intercourse.

170 The Screaming O Vibrating Ring is exceptional in that it's disposable. It slips downs to the base of the penis, fits snugly, and provides a mild vibration that lasts for around thirty minutes. Made of translucent coral silicone with a sensational beaded edge, it stretches to fit. Its mild vibratory effect is surprisingly helpful to appreciative female partners.

171 Let's Get Together is a thick spongy cock ring with a vibrating pearl at the top of the ring just behind a mini vibrating capsule. This gives her extra strong stimulus in exactly the right place, and it feels pretty good for you, too. It comes in brilliant purple and pink gel.

VIBES FOR
both of you

172 The Hitachi Magic Wand is still the Rolls-Royce of vibrators, and is still a bestseller. This enormous, two-speed, plug-in model possesses a sturdy wand handle and a huge vibrating head. What is new about it is that there are now attachments fitting onto the head that focus on clitoral stimulation.

173 Tech Rabbit. This is an improved version of all those other rabbits and a bestseller for Passion8.co.uk.

174 Attachments. What is special about the last two vibrators is that there are some cute pink or purple G-spot attachments that can also be used to give you a prostate massage. Plus one has a slender curved tip specially shaped to give maximum pressure on the front wall of the vagina where your woman's mysterious G-spot is located.

pulsating VIBRATORS

The very latest models don't just vibrate—they do a lot more. The key differences are:

○ **They pulsate, which your woman might recognize as integral to her style of orgasm, especially for G-spot stimulation.**

○ **They are a lot quieter, so you can let rip without alerting the entire household.**

175 The Astro Vibe is thick and phallic. It comes in sinister black with a generous white head, and it's made of soft, skin-friendly ThermoPlastic Elastomer. It sends powerful vibrations from the disc switch control to the tilted head, which has been specifically designed to hit the G-spot better.

176 The Onye vibrator is one of the best pulsating vibrators around. It looks like a neat shiny, black cylinder, rounded at both ends, and it's small enough to be used as a travel accessory. It has a mind-blowing eight speeds of vibration and five separate and different pulsation patterns.

177 Spiral Plug Kit. This is a spiral plug in metallic black that includes a removable itty-bitty vibe, which nestles perfectly into the base. Cord free, this is a quiet and reliable vibrator made of good-quality silicone and is excellent for prostate or vaginal sensation. It uses three watch batteries (included) and has one (strong) speed.

178 I Rub My Duckie. This looks like a rubber duckie, and it floats like a rubber duckie, but when you squeeze the little guy, he buzzes. The ultimate in vibrator disguise. Areas for clitoral stimulation are his beak and tail.

179 Bottoms Up Kit. Available at www.littledeath.com, this kit includes the lavender jelly rubber Arrow Twist Vibe, which probes and promotes thrilling interior sensations. It also comes with batteries and a bottle of special lube.

finger VIBRATION

180 Fukuoku 9000 is one of the most ingenious newer vibrators. Working off tiny watch batteries, it fits over your finger like a tiny finger sheath and vibrates. There is no battery pack and no cord. Perfect for surprises during intercourse, since it is virtually undetectable. The kit includes textured rubber pads to fit over the device so that you can vary your finger sensation.

181 Pocket Rocket is a small rocket-shaped vibrator—a little like a pocket flashlight in appearance. But what transforms it are the wonderful jelly rubber sleeves that fit over it. Comes in lustrous, almost edible colors such as blueberry, grape, lime, strawberry, and tangerine. You can also add jelly rubber sleeves shaped like a bunny (with extra-long ears!) or a variety of nubbly textures.

anal CREATIONS

182 Thai beads. A string of three small pearly-pink beads to be inserted into the anus and then pulled out slowly, to accentuate stimulation, or in a rush, for a thundering climax.

183 Jumbo beads. A graduated larger version.

184 Jelly beads. Spongy ruby-colored, equally sized jelly beads with a ring pull that offers a firm jelly-like sensation.

butt
PLUGS

185   Butt plugs are designed to be worn for the feeling of fullness. They are made in silicone or rubber and are easy to clean. Some butt plugs come with heart-shaped bases, and the silicone is excellent for transmitting vibrations—all you have to do is apply a vibrator to the base. These plugs come in a variety of shapes and sizes. There is:

○ The long, thin, pointed plug

○ The shorter, fatter, slightly curved version

○ The small, squat, fat, beaded version

HANDS *free*

186 The double delight. A variety of two-ended dildos to be worn by heterosexuals when the man enjoys anal penetration.

187 The mini-hummer offers targeted vibration for women who find it hard to come. She wears it strapped into place over the clitoris, held on by an elastic waist strap and leg straps. Great during intercourse because it sets you going, too.

188 Triple Stimulation. This is a cock-ring with a flexible dildo for anal penetration while you penetrate her vagina in the time-honored manner.

All these products can be found on the Internet. (Try www.passion8.co.uk or www.stockroom.com/toys/ or www.condomania.)

THE *rubber* FOLLIES

189 Put a large rubber sheet on the floor. Coat yourself and your partner liberally with massage oil and then conduct a wrestling match in the nude. First one to achieve three holds can ask for any sexual service they want.

190 Sex trick: coat the rubber sheet with oil for more spectacular slippage.

If oil doesn't do it for you, some of the newer sex lubricants may. There is:

191 Sylk. Tasteless, odorless, and non-greasy, Sylk mimics the natural vaginal juices. A free sachet is available for sampling. Especially important, Sylk is safe to be used with condoms.

192 Wet Platinum. This is a top-quality lubricant made by Dr. Johnson. It comes in a sexy black bottle and stays wetter and slipperier for longer than any other lubricant in clinical trials. For use by men and women, it's oil free and may be used with condoms.

193 Durex Play Warmer lubrication provides a warm sensation, and Durex Play Tingling gets you tingling in exactly the right places.

All of these lubricants can be bought from www. passion8.co.uk, www.condomania.com or www. condomsdirect.co.uk.

FUN
lubes

Lubricants come in dozens of flavors and colors. Try:

194 Edible lubes—small gelatin-filled capsules that you bite on during oral sex to flood your partner's genitals with sweet-smelling edible gel.

195 Or chocolate-flavored gel.

196 Or a row of little gelatin pots for flexibility of selection.

197 There are so many different kinds that you are best advised to search two main sites for suggestions. Go to www.annsummers.com or www.goodvibes.com. You can use lubes to spice up the greatest cunnilingus of your woman's life.

five SEXTREMES

198 These days it's getting positively normal to spice up the bedroom with toys. Ann Summers, the British high-street sex-shop chain suggests:

○ Handcuffs, in black leather or pink and fluffy

○ Self-adhesive diamanté tattoos

○ PVC blindfold

○ Kinky heart-shaped bottom paddle

○ Fur collar and lead

○ Nipple chain

restrain yourself, PLEASE

Several U.S. erotica companies revealed that nipple clamps were some of the top sellers.

199 Favorite restraint equipment includes:

- Whips

- Canes

- Paddles

- Cat o' nine tails

- Tackle for tying your partner to the bed or padlocking her to the furniture

200 Double dildo. Want to do something a bit different in bed? A little out of the ordinary? Take a tip from your lesbian friend and invest in a double dildo. What can a heterosexual couple do with one of these? Elementary, my dear Watson. You can insert it into her, while she inserts it into you…! If she then gently moves it inside you, you will find your own G-spot massaged (in the male's case, this is the prostate gland), and believe us, you won't be able to control yourself.

201 It sounds crazy, but try doing something quite bizarre. For example, put on tight-fitting rubber underwear one day before you go in to work. Or snap into a pair of your woman's panties underneath your office suit. The constant awareness of your body and its reactions to the unfamiliar materials can be extremely sensual. Not to mention the overpowering desire to confide in a female colleague about your sensuous undies.

SOMETHING *for sir*

Skin Two (www.skintwo.co.uk) makes exceptional clothes out of rubber and PVC. They are slick, shiny, and skintight. They are also beautifully cut, immensely flattering, and stunningly erotic.

The PVC comes in several new textures. As well as the original PVC, there is a realistic leather-look, a matte version like unpolished rubber, snakeskin, and a slinky, sensational satin finish. Try any or all of these:

202 Glossy rubber underwear in cherry red and black.

203 Skin-tight white rubber jodhpurs with tall, black, shiny boots.

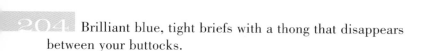

204 Brilliant blue, tight briefs with a thong that disappears between your buttocks.

205 Pièce de resistance—a shiny, black, skin-tight PVC catsuit with a double zip from the front of the neck through the crotch to the base of the spine.

sexual ELECTRICITY

There's the emotional electricity that sparks between you and your woman. But there's also the sort that uses Faraday electricity and bombards her with safe, low-voltage, minilightning bolts. Many of you will have heard of TENS machines, small box-like objects used in physiotherapy, which, by pulsating a tiny electrical charge into the skin, relieve physical pain.

206 There is a sexual version of a TENS machine called the Violet Wand. It's been on sale since the 1930s and is presently enjoying a resurrection of interest. It operates by sending sparks through a single electrode and creates an incredible array of sensations. When held near your body, it sends out a continuous stream of tiny lightning bolts and gives off a distinct purple light. Try kissing while plugged in—better than any spark from a hotel carpet!

207   Available from www1.stockroom.com/fetish/electrical are several sex toys (including the Violet Wand) that use the Faraday principle. There are electrical:

- Butt plugs

- Cock rings

- Vaginal shields

208   Lovemaking in the missionary position while simultaneously using a Violet Wand brings a whole new spark of enthusiasm to an old classic!

safety first— THE RULES

209 Follow the rules:

- Never do anything to anyone against his/her will.

- If you are in doubt, ask or don't do it.

- When playing games of restraint, devise a safety word, which will be strictly adhered to.

- If instinctively you do not trust someone enough to want to play sex games, respect your inner judgment and suggest instead that you and your friend spend more time getting to know each other.

- Ask about AIDS exposure.

- Practice safe sex.

- Do not do anything that would harm anyone.

- Practice birth control.

six | SEXOPOLY

SEX
as art

At the times when we are not actually having sex, many of us like to think about it or even view it.

210 If you want to look at the sumptuous work of illustrator Vargas, you can see it by going to www.eroticart.com.

211 Famous U.S. sex educator Betty Dodson (www. dodsonandross.com) wears another hat as a powerful illustrator of erotic subject matter. Her Leda and the Swan is to die for.

kinky CARDS

212 Send your loved one an ecard—one that's designed to surprise and titillate. Options to choose from on www. kinkycards.com are:

○ Old-fashioned Edwardian pin-up pix.

○ Strange airy-fairy draperies from the 1970s.

○ Very up-to-date kinky humor.

213 Warning: don't forget, it's illegal to send anything deemed obscene through the post office. Hand deliver instead!

TONGUE
twisters

Want to give your woman the most amazing oral sex ever? The secret is to exercise your organ of exquisite pleasure by practicing the following exercises in front of the bathroom mirror at least twice a day for two weeks.

214 Pointing your tongue and pushing it forward a little, flicker it from side to side, keeping up a steady rhythm. Still pointing, flicker it up and down, keeping up a steady rhythm.

215 With a broad tongue, practice lapping, with the focus on the upward movement of the tongue, therefore providing an upward beat.

breast strokes
FOR FOLKS

Offer warm sensual caresses on all parts of your woman's body. Include the breasts in unhurried fashion. Once she is relaxed, coat your warm hands with massage oil and begin.

216 The diagonals. Place your left hand just below and to the left of her left breast, palm downward, your fingers pointing toward her right shoulder. Slowly and without pressure, slide the flat of your hand up and over the left breast diagonally off toward the right shoulder. Before your left hand ends the stroke, start another in the same place with the right hand. Then do the same for the opposite diagonal.

217 The spirals. Coat a warm fingertip lightly with oil, and (with fingernail well trimmed) gently and slowly circle the outside of her breast. On completing each lap, slightly shorten the circle a little so that your finger is effectively climbing a spiral around her breast with the aim of ending at a tiny fixed point on the nipple, having circled it several times first.

218 Sex trick: experiment with different speeds and pressures and don't be afraid to ask which feels best.

219 The crab. With hands bunched in crab-like shapes, place them on one of her breasts, fingertips only, on either side of her nipple, and very slowly draw the hands apart and down the sides of the breast. Repeat for the other breast.

220 Sex trick: don't forget to stroke your partner on every part of her body at every opportunity.

221 The seashore. With both hands bunched in crab-like shapes, place them each on one breast, fingertips only, on either side of her nipples and draw them down in opposite directions until they end diagonally apart, then draw them together again up and diagonally in the opposite direction. This constant together-then-apart motion is intended to feel like the tide going in and out at the seashore.

222 Raspberry nipple. Tell her you have her favorite flavored ice cream on hand and want to feed it to her spoonful by spoonful. What you don't say is that you are a messy boy and will be spilling the occasional dollop en route. Target her nipples. The spillages will need retrieving probably by tongue. Since yours is the nearest one available, it is clearly your duty to use it.

223 Sex trick: make sure you swirl the ice cream all the way around both nipples, a lot.

private FILM SHOW

224. Turn the bedroom into a small cinema. Equip the room with low lighting, a TV screen, a box of chocolates, and a steamy sex film. I'm not talking the rather crude blue sort here. These do turn guys on, but if they are too crude, they turn women right off. This is not what you are aiming at. So see if Netflix or your local video store has:

○ *9 1/2 Weeks*

○ *Ai no corrida*

○ *The Kama Sutra*

lip SYNCHING

Here's where you match your well-tempered tongue to your lover's longing skin.

225 Daisy kisses. Plant small kisses, which contain just a little suction from your lips, all over your partner's body, including behind her and finishing off on the labia.

226 Ice-cream lick. Treat your partner's genitals like a giant ice-cream cone and, using the broad blade of your tongue, lick her in luscious strokes.

227 The lipstick. Moistening part of her body and lavishly moistening your own lips, slide your lips gently backward and forward over the area as if you are applying lipstick.

228 Snake tongue. This is where your tongue twisters come in handy. Rapidly flicker the tip of your tongue across her flesh.

229 Sex trick: work your way up her labia, ending up by flickering across the head of the clitoris.

230 School of sucking. Gently slide your lips, sucking on pathways along your partner's body. Gliding up the inner thigh can be effective because you meet her genitals at the top. You might try sucking gently at each of her labia. Then slide up to her clitoris and suck on it.

231 Repeat the exercise with the further option of flickering your tongue at the same time. Keep moistening your lips.

These tongue strokes are inspired by Ray Stubbs, guru of all types of sensuous massage.

232 In-and-out suction. Suck a nipple, an earlobe, or her clitoris gently into your mouth. Then, while maintaining the suction, push with your tongue so that you are partially but not completely expelling the organ. Then draw the organ back in again. You can practice on your own fingertip to work out the best methods. If you do this with an earlobe, be careful not to make sounds that will blast your loved one's eardrum.

The sexiest positions are not the ones where you swing from a chandelier. Surprisingly, they are the tried-and-true moves but with a few added extras to streamline.

233 Sex from the rear. There's something about sex from the rear that sends the senses of men and women galloping. Perhaps it's because we find ourselves pitchforked back to caveman behavior, but the sight of those rounded moons penetrated by your dancing stick says it all.

234 Sex trick: add your fingers to your partner's clitoris while you take her from behind.

235 The missionary plus. Do you know why the missionary position became an all-time favorite? The answer: it works so well on a lot of levels. It allows face-to-face contact, which means we can look each other erotically in the eye. It provides skin-to-skin full frontal contact, which is incredibly arousing, and even if female climax is a bit hit and miss, it works a lot better orgasmically than, say, sex from the rear.

236 Sex trick: add your fingers or one of these new slender vibrating probes to the act so that her clitoris gets the attention it deserves, which, sadly, intercourse alone does not provide.

STOP
gaps

237   Some seriously sexy women adore anal stimulation. Some enjoy as many fingers as you care to insert. But most of us are so influenced by rigorous cleanliness training as children that we find it hard to believe that anal play might be acceptable. So we don't make the special moves that many women would welcome. Yet there are ways now of introducing anal play as part of the heterosexual experience.

238   Try using a butt plug during intercourse next time the two of you get together. These are available in graduated sizes and a variety of shapes (check the Internet). If you or your woman is anxious about first time usage, invest in the smallest size, which will be the easiest to insert. Some also vibrate.

239 Sex trick: don't surprise your woman with this. Please be certain she will welcome the notion. Otherwise your move might feel like assault, which would definitely not be a good idea.

240 Note: trim all fingernails or use surgical gloves and loads of lubes for any serious anal handwork.

future APHRODISIAC

So what are the future attractions in the shape of orgasm inducers?

The newest experiment in sex sensations of the future comes in the shape of a black Lycra catsuit. It fits snugly with electrodes attached at the breasts, crotch, and other sensitive locations. The suit is designed to plug into a computer's printer port, and the idea is that it will let the user reach out over the Internet and touch someone in a very special way. By clicking on the appropriate parts of an on-screen body image, a remote partner will be able to send stimulating sensations—such as heat, feather touch, or vibration—directly to the suit wearer's wired erogenous zones. Sounds wonderful doesn't it? So far, the idea is only at the experimental stage.

The website www.passion8.co.uk reports that all the Fleshlight ranges top their bestseller lists. These are very soft, realistic replicas of women's orifices in pale fleshy pink at the head of a flashlight-shaped container. They come with several variations, such as the ice-cold version.

One of the greatest innovations for good couple sex comes in the shape of the We Vibe. This is a small, purple, U-shaped vibrator that gives both clitoral and G-spot stimulation during penetration. The speed of vibration can be moderated and ranges from mild to thrilling, and while it feels sensational for both partners, it can help a partner with mild orgasm inhibition because it intensifies her feelings. Available from www.sh-womenstore.co.uk.

242 Do not play any sex games with someone you distrust or someone you have only just met.

243 Both of you must be willing. It is out of the question to force games on someone who, say, has claustrophobia. Or indeed to force games on anyone.

244 Agree on an emergency word or phrase, which is your safety code, which you KNOW will always be respected.

245 Do not attempt any games with someone in poor health.

246 Do not restrict airways or use tight restraints that prevent proper circulation.

gaming PROPS

247 Be subtle. Start light bondage games by using simple items such as a silk scarf, tights, or a necktie.

248 Buy a sleep blindfold. It can be used for having a quiet night and then for having a really exciting one.

249 Squares of silk, satin, and fur are amazing secret weapons.

250 Top up with warm massage oil and possibly with ice cubes!

JUDGING YOUR
partner's mood

As you can probably imagine, it might be disastrous to advance upon your lover with a silken rope only to discover that she can't even cope with oral sex, let alone anything more daring.

251 Get to know your partner well. Talk about how far each of you would like to go. This is easier done at the start of a relationship.

252 Sex trick: talking about your desires to get into gaming can be an erotic buildup in itself, provided your partner is like-minded.

provoking AND TANTALIZING

253 As you stroke and caress (as you would at the start of any lovemaking, of course), build a picture in words of how you most enjoy touching and stroking her most secret recesses, but don't exactly match the words with actions. Stroke near but not on the places she most wants you to touch. The key to success is "frustration of expectation."

254 Sex trick: get her used to you not touching her most sensitive zones, then accidentally let one finger wander and trail ever so lightly across the genitals. If you are doing it properly, she should gasp.

RAISING THE *temperature*

255 Now you want to suggest to your partner that it's time for a little extra surrender: "Would you like to feel unlimited pleasure, to go almost crazy with desire?" you might inquire. "You would? Then keep your hands over your head while I get to work."

the TAKEOVER

256 It's very difficult to keep your hands over your head while being teased just off center below the waist, so your lover is likely to disobey. Now you suggest a little help in keeping her hands out of the way: "Let me just bind your hands together with this silk scarf."

257 Sex trick: on this first occasion, remember—less is more. As you tie the knots you might whisper: "Relax. Forget the day; forget where you are; lose yourself; don't think about me; let your mind wander where it will and visit that secret erotic place only you know about and can enter." All the while make your caresses more persistent and feather-light.

the BLINDFOLD

258 Hint in a subdued voice how it might be fun for your partner to close her eyes, to see nothing, to float into darkness and focus on her dreams, and suggest she could find this easier if she borrowed your bedside blindfold.

FORFEITS

This could consist of caressing your woman and forbidding her to utter any sounds of appreciation. If she forgets, she has to tolerate:

259 A mild spanking.

260 An ice cube pressed to the navel.

261 Her nipples tweaked.

262 Sex trick: the secret here is to pretend she has erred even when she has not.

263 In the red museum. You are an exhibit and your dream partner is blindfolded. She has to identify you through caressing your naked body, and you cannot move, regardless of where she touches.

264 The seven veils. A beautiful slave is brought to the auction block swathed in cloaks and scarves. The cruel slave master slowly peels these away as he describes exactly what he plans to do to the slave. Beneath the cloaks are many thin veils. For each veil that is ripped off, the slave is ravished.

265 The high-class hooker. Your partner is a high-class hooker. You, as her client, must tell her exactly what you want her to do. Every time she finishes one activity she must ask for the next command. You continue until one of you can go no farther.

266 Torture by tickling. Literally what it sounds like. Bind your partner (loosely) to the bed, then target her most sensitive areas. Ensure that your touch is extremely light and moves rapidly, like a spider darting. Most ticklish areas: feet, belly, armpits, inner thighs, around the breasts.

267 Play at pornographers. If you have your own video camera and PC editing suite, make your own "blue" movie. Then watch it together from your bed.

A word of warning: if there is any likelihood your partner is not trustworthy, don't do it. Intimate pictures have been known to show up on people's computers on the other side of the world.

268 Sitting in the backseat. Drive out to a secluded place and move to the back seat. In spite of the inconvenience and the cramps, the sheer unfamiliarity of the surroundings gets you moving at up to 100 mph.

BE
cautious

269 Be loving and do not rush things. Be ready to switch back into a more conventional mood the minute your partner indicates she wants this. The entire success of this sort of game depends on the rapport that the two of you strike up. You must tune in to her mood for games of restraint and domination to work. If she goes cold on you, stop immediately. But once the two of you have agreed, what are the blindfold games you might enjoy?

Anne Hooper and Phillip Hodson are the coauthors of more than a dozen bestselling sex guides, including *How to Make Great Love to a Woman, Anne Hooper's Kama Sutra, Anne Hooper's Pocket Sex Guide, Great Sex Games,* and the *KISS Guide to Sex.* They are psychotherapists and renowned sex therapists who have helped thousands of couples. They have been life partners for more than twenty-five years, and they live together in England.